Original title:
Sprouting Ideas

Copyright © 2025 Creative Arts Management OÜ
All rights reserved.

Author: Riley Hawthorne
ISBN HARDBACK: 978-1-80581-801-4
ISBN PAPERBACK: 978-1-80581-328-6
ISBN EBOOK: 978-1-80581-801-4

Dawn of Inspiration

In a garden where thoughts take flight,
Seeds of wisdom bloom in delight.
A squirrel's dance, ideas take shape,
Juggling clouds, a comical scrape.

Daffodils chuckle, tulips tease,
Sunshine tickles the bumblebees.
Dreams bounce like balls in a game,
Whispers of laughter, no two the same.

Petals of Possibility

A flower pot filled with wild prose,
Daisies laugh while the garden grows.
Bees wear sunglasses, sipping sweet tea,
As butterflies flutter, oh so carefree.

Each petal a thought that tickles the mind,
Ideas, like children, run wild, unconfined.
Jokes sprout up like weeds in their glee,
Nature's own stand-up, just wait and see.

Chasing the First Light

Chasing beams through the morning mist,
A cat in a hat can't resist.
Ideas race like rabbits on a track,
Silly thoughts, there's no looking back.

Roses in sneakers, running so fast,
The dawn of laughter, bright and vast.
Tickles of sunlight on leaves and eyes,
In this race, there are no goodbyes.

Fragments of a Dreamscape

In a dream where giggles collide,
A cloud takes a swim on a colorful slide.
Puppies in pajamas, a sight so rare,
Each thought a bubble, floating in air.

Dancing raindrops drop with finesse,
Silly sombreros on the sky's dress.
Every fragment of whimsy, a laugh on display,
In this landscape of dreams, we merrily play.

Echoes of Inspiration

In a mind like a blender, ideas swirl,
Thoughts start to dance, give a twirl.
A napkin's scribble, a doodle divine,
Turns a simple laugh into a grand design.

Coffee spills and crumbs from toast,
Give birth to musings I love the most.
Jokes laced with truth pop and fizz,
Like jellybeans in a fridge, oh what a whiz!

The Fabric of Discovery

A patchwork quilt of silly schemes,
Stitched together with laughter and dreams.
Got a sock puppet that sings in the rain,
With every note, it loosens the brain.

A bingo card of thoughts gone wild,
Ideas create chaos, like a hyper child.
Pulling at threads, I find something neat,
Who knew a sock could make my heart beat?

The Awakening Mind

A rooster crows, my brain's in flight,
Mimics a squirrel, just out of sight.
Ideas peck like birds on the ground,
With each quirky twist, new thoughts abound.

Head full of bubbles, a fizzy delight,
Chasing them down feels oddly right.
I juggled my brain with marshmallow fluff,
Who knew that thinking could be so tough?

Serendipitous Seeds

Planting thoughts like seeds in spring,
Watering with giggles, oh what a thing!
A tangle of laughter, they grow and twist,
In the garden of nonsense, how could I miss?

Ideas bloom like daisies in sun,
Each one quirky, each one fun.
A banana peel here, a pie in the air,
Oh, what a harvest, catch if you dare!

The Arc of Aspiration

In a garden of thought, ideas bloom,
Like daisies in sunlight, dispelling the gloom.
With each quirk and twist, they dance all around,
Tickling the brain, making laughter resound.

One sprightly notion wore a green hat,
Swapping wisdom for chocolate, now that's where it's at!
With giggles and grins, they all take a leap,
Sowing wild visions, it's a secret to keep.

Illuminated Pathways

On pathways of whimsy, ideas take flight,
Drawing maps in the stars, what a marvelous sight!
With bubbles of laughter, the mind starts to race,
Creating a website for each funny face.

The squirrels join in, wearing tiny bow ties,
Planning a party where pizza fills the skies.
Confetti of thoughts, like fireworks at night,
Chasing the shadows, embracing the light.

The Alchemy of Dreams

In the cauldron of whimsy, ideas collide,
A sprinkle of laughter, a whimsical ride.
With unicorns breaking the rules of the game,
Mixing up nonsense, it's never the same.

Elixirs of giggles, brewed strong and bright,
Transforming the mundane into sheer delight.
With bubbles of magic, our dreams take the stage,
Turning echoing thoughts into a funny page.

Rooted in Vision

With roots of good humor, thoughts dig in deep,
Blooming bright stories that dance in our sleep.
Like clowns in a circus, ideas arise,
Twirling and spinning, what a grand surprise!

These seeds of invention, oh how they grow,
Sprouting wild notions like a comical show.
In the garden of giggles, our dreams intertwine,
Harvesting laughter, pure joy, and good wine.

Echoes of the Heart

In a quiet room, my thoughts wed,
A dance of ideas in my head.
Why did the lamp get so bright?
It whispered secrets all night.

The cat started to think aloud,
Wonders that made him feel proud.
He pondered deeply about fish,
And where they'd go if they could wish.

A chicken laid some plans at dawn,
Wrote a novel on the lawn.
It cock-a-doodle-doodled fun,
And plotted stories 'til it won.

The floor was shaking with delight,
As scribbles turned to flight.
Who knew that dreams had such flair?
Behind each door, madness everywhere.

The Orchard of Opportunity

In a garden where thoughts will bloom,
Ideas dance and clear the room.
With every fruit, a new tale grows,
Like apples fresh with hidden prose.

A squirrel read a book one night,
Thought he could become a knight.
He grabbed a nut, a sword of fate,
And marched around feeling great.

The flowers giggled, swayed with glee,
At the nutty knight beneath the tree.
They whispered plans for a grand parade,
With every glance, new dreams were laid.

Butterflies wore tiny hats and ties,
Telling jokes that caught the skies.
In this orchard, laughter's the key,
As every blossom sings with glee.

Rebirth of Concepts

A toaster had a stroke of luck,
Decided it would run a muck.
With every pop and every toast,
It dreamed of being a bread-lover's ghost.

The blender wished to take a trip,
To blend with smoothies on a ship.
It whirled and twirled with great finesse,
Creating flavors, nothing less.

A fridge conspired with a fan,
To throw a party for the pantry clan.
A salsa dip with cool salsa moves,
Turned leftovers into groovy grooves.

Then light bulbs flickered, inspired by cheer,
They plotted to make a bright idea sphere.
In this zaniness, wisdom's the start,
As every thought plays the jokester's part.

Melodies of the New

A banjo sat dreaming of a show,
Thought it could dance to a country flow.
With every pluck, a giggle charmed,
The audience laughed, completely disarmed.

Clocks ticked and tocked in delight,
As minutes joined to dance all night.
They swung their hands, a rhythmic beat,
Every hour brought a new retreat.

A suitcase began to waltz on its own,
Yearning for travels, longing to roam.
It shimmered and shook with every spin,
Inviting wanderlust to come within.

In this symphony of whimsy and cheer,
Ideas jived, bringing joy near.
With laughter as the sweetest sound,
New melodies of life abound.

Shadows of Potential

In a garden where thoughts take flight,
Ideas bloom in morning light.
Fuzzy logic gets tangled in vines,
While laughter waltzes with playful signs.

A seed once pondered, what to be,
An apple tree or banana spree?
It cracks a joke while sprouting leaves,
Tickling dreams, oh how it believes!

Roots are whispering comedic tales,
Of squirrels plotting while nothing fails.
The tulips giggle as they sway,
In the breeze of thoughts, come what may.

So here in this patch of bright delight,
Unruly dreams dance day and night.
Each notion a petal, soft and fine,
In the garden where minds intertwine.

Paradox of Growth

A cactus says, "I don't need rain,"
While dandelions plot on the windowpane.
"Who needs sunlight when I have shade?"
But in the dark, the fun is made!

Underneath a rock, ideas play hide and seek,
Giggles resonate, they dance and squeak.
A gnarled old tree confesses with glee,
"I sometimes wish to be a bee!"

Growth is a riddle, a topsy-turvy game,
Like trying to choose your own name.
"Should I be tall, or swim-like a fish?"
A salad of thoughts, a zany dish!

With roots interspersed and branches wide,
The wise old owl just shrugs and sighed.
The paradox of growth leads us to jest,
Embrace the nonsense, it's for the best!

The Foliage of the Mind

In the forest of ideas, leaves swirl and spin,
Each thought a twig, join the din.
Hilarity blooms like daisies in spring,
Frolicking notions, what joy they bring!

The acorn chuckles, "I'm not too small,"
While dreaming of being the biggest of all.
A worm bursts forth, with tales to share,
"Let's giggle about growth, if you dare!"

Branches sway as whispers ensue,
"Why not grow legs and dance too?"
With every twist, the humor lies,
In the foliage of dreams, the laughter flies.

So climb aboard this wacky vine,
Where thoughts grow wild and intertwine.
Planting jokes in the fertile mind,
The laughter echoes, uniquely unconfined!

Cradled Inspirations

Bouncing thoughts in a cradle swing,
Ticklish notions that joyfully cling.
Whimsical wishes in the air, oh my!
Ideas play hopscotch, bouncing high!

A cloud draped laughter, floating by,
Sipping sunshine with a lemon pie.
"Why not dream big?" a leaf chirps light,
"We could be stars shining bright tonight!"

The roots take a nap, all snug beneath,
While dreams turn into a playful wreath.
A giggle erupts from the soil so deep,
As visions and laughter gently creep.

In this garden where humor grows,
Every sprout a punchline that glows.
Cradled inspirations, all in a row,
Let out your chuckles, let them flow!

Dancing with Possibility

In a world where thoughts twirl and sway,
Ideas leap like kids in May.
Juggling notions, I take a chance,
With every giggle, I join the dance.

Bouncing bubbles of quirky dreams,
Chasing laughter, or so it seems.
My thoughts parade in mismatched shoes,
Beneath the disco ball of my muse.

Each notion spins, a silly sight,
Twirling round, oh what delight!
With every hiccup, fresh minds collide,
In the joyous chaos where I reside.

So come and laugh, join the fun,
In the carnival of ideas, we run.
With a wink and a nudge, we all partake,
And dance with a flourish, for laughter's sake!

The Undercurrent of Ideas

Underneath the surface, bubbles rise,
Thoughts float whimsically like fireflies.
A splash of chaos, a sprinkle of glee,
Ideas frolic like fish in the sea.

Tickling the mind like a playful breeze,
Wiggly visions that aim to please.
Caught in currents with giggles galore,
I dive in deeper; who knows what's in store?

Some ideas flop, like fish out of stream,
Yet others soar, fulfilling the dream.
With a wink and a nod, we softly tease,
Sharing secrets like whispers from trees.

So let's ride the waves, let our thoughts run wild,
Caught in the funnel, like a joyful child.
In the undercurrent, we laugh and play,
As ideas swirl and drift away!

Champagne of Creativity

Pop the cork, let the bubbles fly,
Ideas fizz like stars in the sky.
With each sip, imagination blooms,
Tickling senses like party balloons.

Laughter mixes with sparking cheer,
Sipping dreams, oh the joy is near!
Pouring visions in a colorful glass,
Swirling thoughts, like guests at a class.

Some overflow, a bubbly surprise,
While others dance, twinkling eyes.
With a splash and a giggle, we toast to the night,
To every wacky wonder that feels just right.

So raise your glass to the wild and free,
To the zany notions, let's shout with glee!
In the champagne of thoughts, let's find our spark,
As the corks pop, we light up the dark!

A Cascade of Fresh Thoughts

In a garden of rubber ducks,
Thoughts bubble up like fizzy drinks.
With every twist of a playful quack,
New ideas bounce back from the brink.

Jellybeans dance in a quirky line,
While cupcakes wear hats of spun sugar,
Laughter blooms like wildflower's shine,
As ideas take flight—they just can't linger!

A pancake flips with a goofy grin,
Swinging ideas like a child at play.
Sticky fingers on the chin,
Queasy giggles come out to stay.

And thus, in chaos, dreams unwind,
With each twist, what joy we find!
In this quirky quest, we're aligned,
Who knew fun thoughts could be so unconfined!

Echoes of Bright Fantasies

A parrot sings in polka dots,
Ideas swirl like confetti rain.
With giggles shared in funny knots,
Silly dreams crack up the mundane.

Kites made of cheese fly high above,
With tunes of laughter in the air.
Thoughts waltz like owls in love,
Spinning tales without a care.

Balloons whisper secrets untold,
As pudding cups spin in delight.
We find the fun in colors bold,
Chasing thoughts into the night.

Echoes bounce like rubber balls,
Every chuckle a bright refrain.
In this merry world, joy sprawls,
Let the beats of laughter entertain!

The Crucible of Creation

Stir the pot with a spoon of glee,
A dash of giggles, a pinch of zest.
Ideas bubble, look at me!
In this cauldron, we're simply blessed.

Waffles shaped like a happy cat,
Twirl and tumble with every bite.
Colors clash like a jazzy hat,
Ideas frolic, feeling just right.

Under cupcakes with funny faces,
New thoughts bloom like candy flowers.
As we tumble through quirky places,
Creativity plays for hours.

In the crucible, we start to dance,
Mixing dreams like a silly stew.
With every jig, we take our chance,
To catch the joy in what we do!

Flickers in the Fog

Through the mist, a thought takes flight,
A glowworm giggles, lighting the dark.
Funny shadows dance with delight,
    As ideas ignite—a merry spark.

Marshmallow clouds drift around with grace,
    While jellyfish wiggle in the fog.
Thoughts bubble up, join the race,
As laughter echoes like a friendly hog.

Pumpkins roll with a cheeky grin,
Whispers escape between the trees.
Silly notions waltz within,
As ideas float like a gentle breeze.

Flickering thoughts emerge in play,
With each giggle, we light the way.
In the fog, fun refuses to stray,
Together we dance—the night's bouquet!

Whispers of New Beginnings

In the garden of my brain,
Thoughts like weeds, they twist and twine.
Chasing sunbeams, dodging rain,
One bright spark, and all is fine.

Giggles pop like tiny seeds,
Growing up with wild requests.
"Hey! What if we dance with weeds?"
Or ride a snail to thought contests?

Butterflies on coffee breaks,
Swapping jokes with dandelions.
A tickle here, a giggle wakes,
Mind's mischief, pure confessions!

Frogs in blazers hop with flair,
Wearing dreams like fancy hats.
As ideas float through the air,
Who knew brains could play like that?

Seeds of Thought Unearthed

A kernel bursts from dirty ground,
It whispers secrets, round and stout.
"What if plants wore shoes?" it sounds,
And giggles dance from sprout to spout.

I planted thoughts in coffee pots,
Watered them with silly grins.
They sprout like trees from little dots,
As chattering birds share the wins.

Tangled roots with jolly pride,
Twisting tales and zooming highs.
"What's a veggie's favorite ride?"
Would it be a bus that flies?

Tiny sprouts, they band together,
Each idea a wacky plot.
They wave their leaves, through any weather,
Creating chaos on the spot!

The Blooming of Concepts

Petals burst in pots of thought,
As giggles sprout from silly dreams.
"What if spoons could hold a plot?"
They'd turn the world into ice creams!

In the meadow of my mind,
Unruly blossoms shake and twist.
Daffodils are not so blind,
They bloom with each absurdist twist.

Promises of candy skies,
Filled with laughter, chirpy glee.
"Bananas can sing lullabies!"
Imagine that, what joy to see!

Funky blooms with socks and ties,
Strutting thoughts that paint the day.
With a wink, their brilliance lies,
As giggles lead the grand ballet!

Tender Tendrils of Imagination

In the nook of a whispering tree,
Ideas stretch their leafy arms.
"Can marshmallows ride the sea?"
They giggle loud, disarm the charms.

Venus flytraps play charades,
Guessing what the petals mean.
Thoughts like confetti, brightly made,
Tickle funny bones, unseen.

A squiggly line between the thoughts,
Wiggling pinks and neon greens.
"Do fish wear hats? What've we brought?"
Adventures sprout in silly scenes.

Tendrils curl with a cheeky grin,
Each thought a dance, a playful jest.
What fun to see where thoughts have been,
In the garden where jokes invest!

Unveiling Ideas

In a garden of thoughts, I found a seed,
It giggled and wriggled, oh what a deed!
With a sprinkle of puns and a dash of cheer,
It bloomed into laughter, drawing us near.

Jokes were its petals, so bright and so funny,
Bees danced around, humming sweet like honey.
Each idea took flight, with a quirk and a twist,
In this comedic plot, there's no way to resist.

The more I would water, the funnier it grew,
With each little sprout, came a joke that was new.
I plucked at the leaves, they let out a bleep!
These ideas were ticklish, and oh, what a leap!

Now my thoughts have formed a zany brigade,
Each idea a character, in laughter I wade.
In this garden of giggles, I'm the jesting king,
With every bright notion, I laugh as they sing.

Fountains of Creation

From a fountain of wit, ideas do splash,
They bubble and fizz, oh what a mad dash!
With humor as water, it spills out in streams,
Creating a ruckus, fulfilling our dreams.

The fountains are gushing with nonsense galore,
Each droplet a punchline, we bellyache more.
I stood to gather, a bucket in hand,
Collecting the laughter that's wildly unplanned.

As I poured out the jokes, they soared to the sky,
Some tumbled, some stumbled, but none would deny.
In this pool of delight, we swim and we float,
Launched by hilarity, on a whimsical boat.

So let's splash in the fountains, let creativity flow,
With each twist and turn, let the chuckles bestow.
For out of the water, our humor will rise,
As ideas entwine, beneath giggling skies.

The Web of Imagination

In a web spun of whimsy, ideas do cling,
Like silly old spiders, prancing and swing.
Threads of the quirky, they tangle and tease,
While caught in this network, I laugh with such ease.

Ticklish and sneaky, the notions skedaddle,
Tangled in laughter, my mind's a bright saddle.
Each flick of a thought sends my giggles aflare,
These pliable dreams float like feathers in air.

Bouncing around on this jokey old net,
With each playful twist, why there's no room for fret!
I catch a few phrases, all tied up in knots,
Ideas snicker together, in humorous spots.

So swing on this web, grab your giggles and rhyme,
In the tangle of laughter, now's truly the time.
For what's woven with joy brings a smile to the eye,
In the heart of imagination, we dance and we fly.

Threads of Inspiration

With threads of pure nonsense, I weave and I spin,
A tapestry bright with the laughs tucked within.
Each quip a bright color, each pun a fine stitch,
Creating a blanket that's cozy, not rich.

The loom of my mind clacks merrily away,
As ideas unravel, come join in the play.
With a flick of my wrist, I swing jokes through the air,
And weave them together with a flamboyant flair.

Each thread tells a story, both silly and bold,
Adventures of laughter, like treasures of gold.
So gather your fibers, let's craft something neat,
With threads of amusement, we'll dance on our feet.

In this colorful fabric, we find endless fun,
Ideas intertwined, we'll bask in the sun.
Threads of inspiration, let's twist and combine,
For life's better shared with an extra dose of shine.

Kaleidoscope of Possibility

Colors twist in wacky ways,
Each thought's a dance, a silly craze.
Like noodles bouncing off the wall,
Who knew ideas could jump and crawl?

Rainbows pop from noodle spouts,
What's a dream without some doubts?
A cupcake here, a shark on skis,
Oh look, a llama plays the keys!

Ideas spin like tops in glee,
A monkey juggles, can't you see?
With every twist, a giggle grows,
Who knew thought seeds could wear clothes?

Zooming past like rocket ships,
Each notion flips and does some flips.
In this world of wacky sights,
Join the party, and hold on tight!

The First Light of Ideas

A bulb flickers with a grin,
What wacky thought's gonna begin?
A penguin wearing silly hats,
Or tacos that dance with the cats?

The toaster pops, it spits out dreams,
With butter and jam, or so it seems.
Giggles bounce like rubber balls,
Ideas bounce off kitchen walls!

Who knew that fluff could be profound?
A pancake sings, its voice unbound.
With each new thought, a chuckle flows,
Like custard pools in every prose!

Lightbulbs twinkle, sparks take flight,
Ideas wiggle with pure delight.
In this space, the fun abounds,
Where every laugh is joy unbound!

Echoing Horizons

Bouncing thoughts like rubber ducks,
One weird notion leads to stuck lucks.
Why did the chicken cross the cheese?
To see a cow dance 'neath the trees!

Oh, the echoes of silly giggles,
Ideas prance, and the heart juggles.
Socks with stripes can surely fly,
If seagulls wear them, oh my my!

Chasing rainbows, we might trip,
As cupcakes bounce and on dreams they sip.
Laughter ripples through the air,
What a world must be out there!

Each notion shouts from mountain tops,
With bouncing bunnies and wiggly hops.
In this realm of cheerful sounds,
The laughter of ideas compounds!

The Blooming Mindscape

Watch as thoughts begin to sprout,
Like flowers blooming, silly clouts.
A dandelion in a hat,
Dancing with a whimsied cat!

Balloons that giggle in the sky,
Tickle the brains, oh my oh my!
Conversations like popcorn pop,
What's that giraffe doing on top?

Ideas grow like vines of cheese,
Twisting round legs in a breeze.
A chimichanga on a bike,
Now that's a thought that we all like!

With each new bloom, a laugh will bloom,
As silly notions fill the room.
In this vibrant, quirky space,
Every idea finds its place!

Awakening the Abstract

In a dusty old attic, thoughts collide,
A potato with glasses began to confide.
He whispered of dreams shaped like cheese,
As squirrels in bow ties danced with ease.

The lightbulb flickered, then blinked in surprise,
While a rubber ducky took to the skies.
Pasta noodles drew plans on the wall,
A wild, wavy dance—oh, what a ball!

A cactus took notes, oh so astute,
While the desk lamp hummed a jazzy flute.
Together they laughed, ideas like balloons,
As the clock chimed softly, a tune for buffoons.

The Legacy of Vision

A fish in a hat held a management talk,
While a wall clock tried to mimic the walk.
Everbright jellybeans started to scheme,
For a world made of gumdrops—oh, what a dream!

Graduation caps flew to the ceiling,
As hotdogs debated the meaning of feeling.
Chairs had a meeting, they sat on the ground,
With all those ideas, not a dull moment found!

The toaster applauded with even a pop,
While the cat in the corner said, "Let's not stop!"
A vision of sugar finally arose,
As donuts took stand-up—who knew they could pose?

Whispers of Discovery

A garden gnome measured the dreams of a bee,
While shoelaces tangled in playful decree.
A cupcake with sprinkles skated down the lane,
Chasing after giggles and ice cream rain.

Kites made of wishes danced on a breeze,
While calculators argued about peas.
Together they tossed around wild inventions,
With hiccups and hiccuped by funny tensions!

The moon made a bet with a planet named Lou,
Claiming that stars would be funnier too.
As laughter erupted from every design,
A tapestry woven with humor divine.

The Trellis of Thought

A pickle in pajamas set out to explore,
With dreams growing taller than ever before.
Pencils pranced lightly, sketching the way,
While coconuts cheered, ready to play.

A teacup with a tutu took center stage,
As giggles broke free from the wisdom of age.
Invisible bicycles raced through the air,
Learning to fly from a snail with flair!

The ideas entwined like vines in the sun,
A tangled up crew just having some fun.
With hearty laughter that echoed without end,
In the garden of minds, new journeys ascend.

Seeds Beneath the Surface

In the muck, ideas play hide and seek,
Wiggling around like a funky old tweak.
They squirm and they wiggle, they try to break free,
Might just sprout a joke, or a wild melody.

Underneath the soil, they tickle the ground,
They giggle and chuckle, oh what a sound!
A root with a plan, a stem full of glee,
What will they grow into? A laugh or a spree?

Worms whisper secrets, while ants bring the cheer,
As the sprigs start to blossom, no one needs fear.
A great pun emerges, all green and absurd,
What's this? A quip? Oh, it's quite unheard!

Oh, the dance of ideas, it's messy, it's bold,
With laughter and folly, a sight to behold.
In this garden of chuckles, where dreams come alive,
Who knew that a seed could make humor thrive?

Dreamscapes of Thought

In the land of the bizarre, ideas do waltz,
Cactus in tuxedo? Oh, that's just my faults.
Bananas in pajamas, tap dance on the breeze,
Each giggle a sparkle, each chuckle a tease.

Clouds made of cotton candy float overhead,
While zebras in bow ties gossip in bed.
A whimsy parade where the odd is the norm,
Twirling like puppies in a goofy dance storm.

The teapot is whistling a tune in the air,
With each bubbling note, it's a laugh we all share.
Mountains of jellybeans, rivers of cream,
In this realm of the silly, you're free to daydream.

From dreamscapes of thought, let the nonsense arise,
With laughter, we fashion a world that defies.
Let's write on the clouds, have a giggling spree,
In the land of the daft, come with me, come see!

The Labyrinth of Ingenuity

In a maze of ideas, with a twist and a turn,
A squirrel in spectacles looks like it might learn.
It scampers and chirps, leading thoughts in a race,
In this chaotic garden, they're all in one place.

A lightbulb is flipping through books on a shelf,
While a cat wearing glasses reads softly to itself.
The walls are all sticky with bits of great plans,
Like jelly on toast or a dance with no hands.

We stumble through corners, all giggles and grins,
Each junction a riddle, collecting our sins.
What's that? A grand idea? Or just some bad cheese?
In the labyrinth's depths, we can't help but tease.

So let's make a ruckus in this wacky domain,
With laughter as currency, let's go slightly insane.
In a world of creations, where chaos is keen,
We'll navigate nonsense, no need to be mean!

Bursting Buds

A sprout peeks above, tips its hat with a grin,
With petals a-dancing, let the nonsense begin.
Each bud a surprise, like a pop of confetti,
They burst in a giggle, all jolly and pretty.

With colors that shout and fragrances tease,
Funny little creatures smile with ease.
A flower in slippers does a jig on the lawn,
While bees crack up laughing until they're all gone.

As blooming begins, the whole garden observes,
With cheeky little remarks, and quirks in the curves.
Each bloom a comedian, a joke on the breeze,
They drench us in laughter, our hearts they do seize.

So when you see buds, don't just sigh and stroll,
Join in on the fun, let the bright laughter roll.
In a world filled with colors, where humor takes flight,
Every burst of new life brings a reason to light!

Unfolding Whispers of Tomorrow

In a garden of quirky dreams,
Ideas wiggle like wiggly beans.
They pop up with giggles and grins,
Crafting tales where laughter begins.

Each notion takes a silly flight,
Dancing around like a kite in sunlight.
Tickling the brain, they rotate,
Causing chuckles, oh what a fate!

A banana peel slips in the plan,
Turning smartness into a silly span.
With a wink and a nod they bounce,
Ever so witty, they laugh and pounce.

So gather your thoughts, don't be shy,
Let them spill and multiply.
In this wacky world of the mind,
Joyful mysteries are sure to find.

Tapestry of Thought

We weave our thoughts like a fun parade,
With silly arguments, and ideas displayed.
A patchwork quilt of laughter's delight,
Stitched with giggles, oh what a sight!

Nonsense ticks like a cheeky clock,
Wobbling ideas that spin and rock.
In a world where humor leads the way,
Each thought is a joke that wants to play.

A cat in a hat, dancing in shoes,
Whispers of wisdom in quirky hues.
Thoughts tumble like socks in a dryer,
Colliding, exploding, on a wire.

So grab a notion, let's twist and twirl,
In this wild dance, watch ideas unfurl.
With laughter as the thread that binds,
We create a tapestry of funny minds.

Whispers of Potential

In the depths of a daydream, they sway,
Echoes of thoughts that come out to play.
Like squirrels with acorns, ideas burst,
Crafting a universe, all unrehearsed.

Tickling the cheek of the mind's eye,
Creating a ruckus that bounces high.
With every giggle, a notion is born,
In the circus of thought, the fun is adorned.

A balloon filled with passion and cheer,
Drifting on giggles, bringing us near.
Thoughts twirl like confetti in the air,
With whispers of magic everywhere.

So gather your quirks, don't hold them tight,
Let them loose in the broad daylight.
In the orchestra of laughter, join the refrain,
For each silly thought can dance in the rain.

Seeds of Thought

Tiny seeds tucked in the brain,
Spritzed with chaos and a touch of insane.
Each one a giggle, a quirky delight,
Sprouting up laughter like stars in the night.

In the veggie patch of the mind's fun fare,
Carrots of dreams sprout everywhere.
With whispers that dance on a cool breeze,
They wiggle and jiggle, aiming to please.

A cabbage debates with a spud by the wall,
In this zany garden, they all have a ball.
Ideas are veggies, so ripe and prepared,
Growing wild humor, they're fully declared.

So plant your thoughts in this fertile ground,
Water with laughter, let joy abound.
In this garden of silliness, give it a try,
Watch your ideas bloom, oh me, oh my!

Embryonic Echoes

In a dark little corner, ideas collide,
Giggling softly like kids, they can't hide.
They tumble and bounce, never quite still,
Wiggling like worms, what a vibrant thrill!

An egg in the nest, it starts to shake,
Twisting and turning, for goodness sake!
A crack in the shell, oh what a sight,
Out pops a thought, like a bird in flight!

Bouncing ideas like a game of catch,
One's bright and shiny, another's a scratch.
Mixing and matching with flair and zest,
Creating a ruckus, they can't find rest!

So here they dance, in a wobbly trance,
Frolicking freely, oh, what a chance!
Laughing and teasing, it's what they do best,
In this wild party of thought's crazy quest!

Fledgling Fantasies

A thought on the wing, it flutters and flaps,
Wearing a cap and some funny snaps.
It zooms past the fridge, then takes a dive,
Lunch ideas are live — oh, how they thrive!

In a whirlwind of nonsense, they tumble about,
Racing each other with gleeful shout.
Oh, look at them go, like squirrels in a race,
Chasing the cheese, just to lighten the space!

From doodles on napkins to wacky old dreams,
Ideas bubble up like soda with creams.
They bounce off the walls, they bounce off our heads,
Making us giggle before we see red.

So let's keep them flowing, elusive and free,
Like jelly-filled donuts, oh, what a spree!
Fledgling fantasies, full of delight,
Creating chaos, then taking flight!

The Birth of Creation

In a universe wide, ideas are born,
Like kittens at dawn, with mischief sworn.
Teasing and blending, like colors that merge,
They chuckle and wiggle, on the creative verge!

A canvas of chaos, splatters of fun,
Thoughts popping up like a pastry bun.
There's a squirrel with a beret and big sunglasses,
Mixing up visions, oh, he never amasses.

What if we built a castle of cheese?
Or a trampoline that bounces with ease?
Each thought's a little dancer, prancing so spry,
Twisting and turning, oh my, oh my!

So gather your dreams in this circus of flair,
Ride the rollercoaster, don't stop for air!
The birth of creation, a wild jubilee,
Where laughter and whimsy dance joyously!

From Roots to Wings

In a garden of thought, ideas grow tall,
Like broccoli trees playing hide and crawl.
They wiggle their leaves, then twist in the breeze,
Sipping on sunshine, oh, what a tease!

They start as a whisper, a giggle, a blink,
Then bloom into jest, quicker than you think.
With roots in the soil, and wings made of flights,
They soar through the sky on whimsical nights.

From pickled fish dreams to hats made of cream,
Racing through clouds, they leap and they gleam.
Each thought is a kite, soaring high in the air,
Chasing down rainbows with eccentric flair!

So let's plant our visions in the soil of delight,
Water them gently with laughter at night.
From roots to wings, they'll frolic and play,
Creating a ruckus, come join the display!

The Symphony of Ideas

In a world where thoughts take flight,
Ideas dance like birds in bright light.
A tuba toots, a trumpet blares,
While minds compose in brainstorming fairs.

A saxophone sneezes, oh what a sound!
A giggle erupts from ideas unbound.
In the chaos, laughter draws near,
Creating a symphony, oh so clear.

A tambourine jangles, thoughts all around,
While the triangle chimes, in joy we're drowned.
Join the concert, let your thoughts sway,
In this wacky orchestral display!

So grab your batons, let laughter begin,
With every new idea, let's wear a big grin.
In the symphony of minds, we play our part,
With humor and folly, we open our heart.

Tending to the Mind's Garden

In the garden where ideas bloom,
We water thoughts with a sprinkle of plume.
A rubber chicken rests by the root,
While giggly gnomes dance in a suit.

We trim the weeds with silly shears,
As laughter echoes, it calms our fears.
Ideas sprout up, like daisies in rows,
Talk to them kindly, and watch how it grows.

The scarecrow chuckles with a hearty grin,
While butterflies plot and plan to begin.
We plant a few puns in the warm, rich soil,
And dig up the laughs, oh what a toil!

So tend to your garden, don't let it spoil,
With whimsy and wonder, cultivate the toil.
In this fertile haven, joy is the key,
For laughter and planting set our minds free!

Boughs of Brilliance

In a treehouse where ideas reside,
Boughs of brilliance wait to collide.
A squirrel plays chess with a wise old owl,
As giggles echo like a playful growl.

Branches wobbly with concepts galore,
Each nut a thought we can't help but explore.
The leaves whisper secrets of humor and cheer,
As we swing higher, we shed every fear.

A sloth strums a ukulele on high,
While mischief and mirth in the branches fly.
We climb up the trunks of whimsical dreams,
And dive into laughter like kids in streams.

So reach for the boughs, let your spirit ascend,
With each silly notion, let joy be your friend.
In this treehouse of giggles, let worries unwind,
For freedom of thought is the treasure we find!

Fertile Ground for Thoughts

In the soil where ideas take shape,
Fertile ground for thoughts is no cape.
Worms wear glasses, quite wise indeed,
Sharing insights with every deed.

We sprinkle some humor like confetti on top,
As hearty laughter makes our ideas pop.
A garden gnome gives a thumbs-up cheer,
For wacky thoughts that are surely sincere.

Carrots have jokes as they wiggle down low,
While radishes chuckle, putting on a show.
The sun above beams with a giggly glow,
As we dance with our thoughts, all together we grow.

Here in this bloom, creativity's bound,
With each zany twist, new discoveries found.
So plant all your dreams in this whimsical round,
In the fertile ground, let joy be profound!

The Gentle Rise of Ideation

Beneath the surface, giggles bloom,
Ideas wiggle in the darkened room.
Like little sprouts in a quirky dance,
They tickle thoughts with a playful glance.

A lightbulb flickers, what a tease,
A puppet show of thoughts with ease.
With silly hats and shoes too wide,
They wiggle forth, nowhere to hide.

Each thought a wiggly little bug,
Hitching rides on a friendly mug.
They chatter loud, then shush with glee,
In a world where thoughts run free.

So let them play, let ideas roam,
In jumbled chaos, finding home.
A gentle rise, a joyful cheer,
For all the quirks that bring us near.

Flickers of the Yet-to-Be

From the kitchen comes a bubbling pot,
An idea stew, a wobbly splot.
Carrots of humor, broccoli of dreams,
Stirred together in laughter streams.

A candle's light does a jig inside,
Chasing shadows that jump and glide.
Each flicker sparks a whimsy sight,
Dancing on walls, taking flight.

They say that hope wears polka dots,
And silly socks from thrift shop lots.
With pie in the face, they melt away,
All seriousness goes on holiday.

In this circus of yet-to-be,
Balloons of joy float wild and free.
Watch ideas twirl, they cannot be still,
A rollercoaster of quirky thrill.

A Symphony of New Perspectives

In the orchestra of thoughts galore,
A kazoo squeaks, then a trumpet's roar.
Each note a twist, a laugh, a dive,
Creating tunes that come alive.

The cellos hum with a wink and sway,
As violins sneak in the fray.
Trombones slide, making funny faces,
A concert of giggles, a chorus that races.

Harmony strikes like a playful breeze,
Notes flying high, like cheeky bees.
With each crescendo, laughter explodes,
As ideas march in delightful codes.

So grab your flute, your trombone too,
Join the symphony, here's a cue!
New perspectives are all around,
In this melody where joy is found.

Lifting the Veil of Potential

Behind the curtains, secrets play,
Like kittens chasing shadows all day.
A flap and a wiggle, they peek and tease,
As potential prances on tiptoes with ease.

A magician's hat hides a wobbly thought,
Pulling out whimsy, like it's all caught.
Each card drawn flutters with zest,
What's under there? A funny jest!

With giggles and grins, the layers unwind,
Revealing riches of the playful kind.
Like a piñata bursting with candy and cheer,
Good ideas tumble, making us near.

So lift that veil, take a peek inside,
Watch laughter bloom and ideas glide.
In every nook, there's a quirky delight,
Just waiting to pop, oh what a sight!

The Garden of Imagination

In the garden where thoughts like weeds grow,
A cucumber skates, just putting on a show.
Carrots wear coats, they dance in a line,
While broccoli dreams of being fine wine.

The tulips gossip about the sun's rays,
With laughable voices, in funny displays.
Radishes joke, 'We're roots of the ground!'
While peas in a pod share their secrets out loud.

A scarecrow laughs at the crows that conspire,
And whispers to daisies to join in the choir.
The soil's alive with a chuckling breeze,
Tickling thoughts as they swirl 'round the trees.

In this whimsical plot where the wild ideas roam,
Creativity blooms, calling all minds home.
With humor and giggles, it's clear to see,
This garden's the place where we all can be free.

Unfurling Possibilities

A sock puppet dreams of a world in disguise,
A talking shoe tells of new alibis.
Bananas debate on their peeling approach,
While peppers rehearse for their stage debut broach.

The ants have a dance, spinning tales of delight,
As a pineapple juggles, oh what a sight!
Cabbages rolling on wheels made of cheese,
In this crazy land, laughter comes with ease.

Giggling tomatoes crack up on a vine,
While radishes wear hats that are totally fine.
Puzzles and pranks entwined in a cheer,
In this big circus, no room for a sneer!

From quirky ideas that bounce in a ring,
To vegetables swaying, they're ready to fling.
Each thought a balloon, that floats high and bright,
Tickling our minds like stars in the night.

Bright Sparks in the Dark

When the moon comes out with a curious grin,
Ideas start twinkling, they dance from within.
A fish in a hat gives a wink and a nod,
While shadows perform in a funny facade.

The stars play charades, wearing glittery hats,
And banter with crickets, friendly little chats.
A cloud takes a bow, with a shimmy and glide,
While lightning bugs giggle, their laughter untried.

A comet spins tales of adventures untold,
As fireflies whisper, both daring and bold.
Nighttime's a show where the oddballs all shine,
Joking and laughing, where whims truly align.

In this theater of thoughts, so bright and so stark,
Each flash of inspiration ignites like a spark.
With whimsy afoot and silliness rife,
These ideas take flight, breathing humor to life!

When Concepts Take Flight

A paper airplane dreams of a journey so high,
Looping and twirling, beneath the blue sky.
A crayon takes off, scribbling breezy trails,
While sticky notes flutter like whimsical sails.

The light bulb giggles, a radiant joke,
As ideas escape in a happy little smoke.
A pencil rolls over, with a sharp, silly fuss,
Bouncing around just to catch the big bus.

Marshmallows float by, puffed up with delight,
Talking about sugar and sweet little bites.
A candy cane winks, says it's all in good fun,
Together they soar till the day's almost done.

Concepts take flight on this merry-go-round,
Laughing with joy as new thoughts abound.
With giggles galore, they enjoy their grand ride,
In this silly sky, there's nothing to hide!

In the Cradle of Creativity

In a cozy nook, thoughts start to bloom,
Like a sock left out, they fill the room.
A giggle escapes, like a fish with a hat,
   Ideas swim wild, imagine that!

With a wink of a pencil, doodles take flight,
Cartoon clouds giggling, all day and night.
Chasing the wild ones, they giggle and roll,
   Each little spark, a whispering soul.

Tickling the brain like a feather on cheese,
An avalanche of chuckles brings thoughts to their knees.
Watch out for the banana peel, such a fun trap,
One slip of the mind, and it's a whole new map!

In the cradle where silliness grows,
Nonsense and laughter are best friends, who knows?
Mold your laughter into something bright,
   And share that giggle, ignite the night!

Budding Visions

Tiny thoughts wiggle like worms on parade,
Skipping through ideas, where no one feels weighed.
With hats made of lettuce, they twirl and they spin,
Crafting a world where nonsense begins.

A jester awaits, with a quirk in his grin,
Unruly imaginations, where do they pin?
A hopscotch of dreams on a slippery floor,
Thoughts bounce around, and then giggle some more.

Puns pop like corn, sizzling bright,
Jumping through laughter, oh what a sight!
Budding visions burst forth with delight,
Like confetti thrown high, it feels just right.

Tiptoeing on dreams like cats in the night,
Plucking ideas from clouds, oh what a flight!
With a tickle of humor and a smile all around,
Let's plant silly seeds; they'll grow by the pound!

From Soil to Skyline

In patches of thought, lettuce sprigs sway,
A garden of giggles, come out and play!
Giddy little clouds on a marshmallow sky,
Tickling the fancies that sprout oh so spry.

Plotting and planning goes up like a kite,
With whimsies and laughter keeping it light.
Growing up big as the tallest tall tale,
With roots of the funny, we'll surely prevail.

As dreams dig deep, they twist and they shout,
A wacky topiary, there's no need to pout!
We'll water our hopes with lemonade smiles,
Creating a skyline that dances for miles.

So grab that spade and let's dig in the dirt,
Harvesting humor, it never can hurt.
From soil to skyline, let's make a grand show,
Where laughter is planted and joy starts to grow!

The Fertile Mind's Garden

In the garden of thoughts, ideas take root,
Wearing potato sacks, looking quite cute.
They wiggle and jive, like ants on a quest,
Hoping for harvest and silliness blessed.

A sprinkle of giggles, a dash of surprise,
The flora of fun with bright, twinkly eyes.
With laughter as sunlight and joy as the rain,
Each crazy notion does fashion a chain.

We'll plant all the puns, the riddles, the quirks,
In this fertile domain where silliness lurks.
And as blossoms begin, we'll share a good laugh,
Growing whimsies together, let's all do the half!

So grab those ideas, let's churn them around,
In this quirky garden where wonders abound.
With every good giggle, we'll nourish our land,
The fertile mind's garden, forever unplanned!

The Echo of Untold Stories

In the attic where dust bunnies play,
A whisper of stories from yesterday.
The roaches are writing; it's all quite bizarre,
Using a cupcake as their old typewriter star.

A cat in a hat speaks French with a mouse,
While crayons draw maps of a faraway house.
Uncle Larry's left sock starts shouting with glee,
Claiming he's been to a grand jubilee!

Dancing teabags spill secrets anew,
With flavors so wild, you won't know what to brew.
The laughter is echoing all through the night,
As stories unfold in the soft candlelight.

Each item in corners seems eager to share,
Of pirate ships sailing through jellybean air.
So gather your odds and your ends, my dear friend,
In this attic of laughs, the fun will not end.

Roots of Innovation

Down in the garden, a cabbage wears specs,
While radishes plot the next fashion with flecks.
A carrot named Carl invents a new snack,
That's crunchy and munchy, not hard to unpack.

The potatoes debate what's the best way to fry,
With hopes of creating a pizza with pie.
Eggplants are critiquing their skins' shiny glow,
While peppers are dancing in a salsa show.

The lettuce proposes a leafy parade,
As cucumbers rush to design a cool shade.
With roots in the soil and dreams that take flight,
This garden's a playground, oh what a delight!

So come grab a hoe; let's create something new,
In this mad veggie land, where ideas brew.
For every odd thought may sprout and amaze,
In our whimsical world of green leafy ways.

Awakening the Dormant Muse

The muse took a nap in an old rocking chair,
With dreams of wild llamas floating in air.
She woke with a start, tossed her hair in a mess,
And shouted, "Bring snacks! I need fun, not stress!"

Pens in the drawer began to do flips,
Inkwells were laughing; they all needed sips.
The canvas was jumping in colors so bright,
As brushes began to throw tickles of light.

A painting of pancakes flew up on the wall,
Where syrup cascades like a waterfall.
The muse took a swing on a big marshmallow,
Creating a magic that's soft and quite mellow.

So hop on your whimsy, let the laughter flow,
With ideas as sweet as a fresh cookie dough.
The dormant no longer, she now sings with glee,
In a world of imagination, come dance with me.

Fragrant Notions in the Breeze

A bouquet of thoughts is floating around,
With daisies and dandelions dancing abound.
Lilies smell funny; they giggle and tease,
While wind whispers secrets through rustling trees.

The sunflowers nod like they're ready to chat,
While roses wear glasses, looking quite fat.
Ideas take flight like a kite in the park,
Bouncing from flower to bee with a spark.

The lilacs are plotting a fragrant parade,
While tulips play trumpet, all dressed up and played.
With petals and pollen, they burst into cheer,
Inventing new fragrances for all to hear.

So drift on the breeze where the laughter is ripe,
Join in this fresh garden of giggles and hype.
For every small notion, just wait for the tease,
Of fragrant ideas that float in the breeze.

Nurtured Notions

In the garden of my brain, seeds toss,
They wiggle and giggle, oh what a loss!
A thought pops up, like a weed in spring,
Dancing about, oh the joy it brings.

With shoelaces untied, I trip on a plan,
A pie in the sky, and a monkey with a fan.
Ideas collide, like marbles in a bag,
I laugh so hard, I can't help but brag.

Some thoughts are spry, while others are slow,
Like snails on a mission, they put on a show.
I water the wacky, and prune the absurd,
Those tangled-up notions, they flop and they're stirred.

Oh, the chaos that blooms when I write in a rush,
A turtle with roller skates, a mad, crazy hush!
I nurture my notions with playful delight,
By morning, they're dancing, oh what a sight!

The Canvas of Uncharted Thoughts

On a canvas so vast, thoughts paint with a grin,
A splatter of laughter, where silliness begins.
A purple polka-dotted elephant croons,
While a fish in a top hat hums to the tunes.

Brush strokes of giggles, with colors amok,
Inventing mad scenes like a clock without a clock.
My brain is an artist, with ideas to share,
Each canvas a circus, with clowns everywhere.

With splashes of whimsy, I let my mind roam,
A garden of nonsense feels just like home.
Each thought is a kite, soaring high in the air,
Tangled in string, but I just do not care.

As I paint my wild dreams in hues oh so bright,
The laughter erupts like a dog in a fight.
I step back, and notice my masterpiece flow,
The canvas of nonsense, what a bright, fun show!

Horizons of the Unseen

Out at sea in a boat made of bread,
I sail toward horizons where no one has tread.
Jellyfish serve tea, as the sun starts to melt,
And in the waves, all my wild dreams are felt.

Each wave brings thoughts that bubble and burst,
Like popcorn in a pan, first pop, then a thirst.
A dolphin on skis spins a tale that's absurd,
I laugh till I cry at the things I have heard.

The sky paints a picture of clouds shaped like pies,
As I delve into realms where imagination flies.
Oh look, there's a unicorn juggling a bean,
Mirth dances lightly on horizons unseen.

With a wink to the stars, and a shimmy on deck,
I gather my thoughts like a speckled insect.
Navigating the silly, I've grown quite adept,
Finding joy in the nonsense, my heart full of pep!

Mosaic of the Mind

In the puzzle of thoughts, each piece has a quirk,
Dancing around like a silly little jerk.
They fit together in a riotous way,
A zigzagging wonderland that's here to stay.

Each tile is a giggle, each color a shout,
Creating confusion, with laughter no doubt.
From marshmallow clouds to a whale in a suit,
A banquet of nonsense, where flounders compute.

With marbles and spools, I craft my domain,
A merry mosaic, no drop of disdain.
I might trip on a jester, or wiggle with glee,
This chaos of brilliance is a treasure for me.

So here's to the fragments, the wild that we find,
In the mosaic of laughter, we twirl and unwind.
Like confetti of thought flying high in the sky,
I chuckle at notions that happily fly!

Moments of Insight

In the middle of a snack,
A thought jumps on my back.
Should I share my cookie?
Or just laugh at this rookie?

Ideas skip like a stone,
Bouncing on thoughts full-blown.
What if socks wore shoes?
Oh, the chaos and the blues!

An orange danced with glee,
Wishing it could be a tree.
But then it rolled away,
To join the fruit buffet!

When my cat thinks she's wise,
Staring at the nighttime skies.
Maybe she knows a thing,
About the joy dreams bring.

Stirring the Soul

On a rainy day I ponder,
As the raindrops cause me to wonder.
What if fish could fly?
Would they catch the clouds up high?

With a wink and a grin,
Let's create a world of spin.
Where marshmallows grow tall,
And candy canes paint the wall!

A banana sings a tune,
As it waltzes with the moon.
Can fruit throw a dance fest?
I'd say that's truly the best!

With giggles all around,
Joy and laughter abound.
Let's chase the silly thoughts,
And see what laughter's got!

Cascades of Creativity

In my garden of the mind,
Weeds of worry, I'll leave behind.
Planting seeds of pure glee,
Where squirrels debate philosophy.

A rubber duck on a swing,
Claims to be a world-class king.
As bubbles float and swirl,
Ideas twirl and unfurl.

Pasta noodles taking flight,
Pasta land in pizza night.
Oh, what wild dreams we chase,
When noodles race at their pace!

With a giggle and a dash,
Thoughts collide in a mad splash.
Who knew my thoughts could grow?
Like a rainbow in the snow!

The Nest of Thought

In a tree made of cheese,
Ideas come and go with ease.
Birds chirp tunes of delight,
While squirrels plot in the night.

A pancake dreams of the sky,
Wishing it could soar and fly.
Despite the syrupy plight,
It laughs and spins, what a sight!

With giggles from a snail,
Who races in a tiny trail.
What if he wrote a book,
On how to cook with a hook?

Thoughts come home to nest,
In the warmth of laughter's zest.
Each silly whim on cue,
Brings joy in shades of blue!

Harvesting Creativity

In fields of mind, thoughts grow tall,
Like popcorn kernels, they spring and sprawl.
Some jump high, while others trip,
A wobbly dance, a silly zip.

With laughter loud, we gather round,
To pick the ones that leap and bound.
A scattering of quirks, a mix of fun,
In the garden where ideas run.

Each thought's a fruit, both sweet and odd,
Like jellybeans sprouting from the sod.
We pluck them fast, not giving pause,
For in ridiculousness, there's applause.

So let's all tend this vibrant patch,
Where dreams of jelly creatures match.
In our harvest, we'll find delight,
Silly and bright, oh what a sight!

In the Cradle of Thought

In a cradle made of chuckles, thoughts like jellies sit,
Wobbling and giggling, they just won't quit!
A wild parade of what could be,
Floating on clouds, oh what a spree!

Ideas frolic like puppies at play,
Chasing their tails, then running away.
Who knew a thought could roll this fast?
Bouncing and leaping, they'll never last!

A ticklish breeze whispers loud and clear,
"Don't let them wander too far, my dear!"
So we gather the giggles and knot them tight,
Creating a quilt of pure delight.

In this cradle of whimsy, the fun never fades,
Each thought a wild dance in jazzy parades.
Laughter and wonder in a merry swirl,
Ideas take flight, let imagination twirl!

Cultivating Innovation

With gardening gloves, we plant our dreams,
Watering ideas with spritz, not screams.
A sprinkle of giggles here and there,
Watch them blossom, unaware!

In our patch of wonder, come see the rows,
Of funky concepts that tickle the toes.
A whacky zucchini laughs in glee,
While a cantaloupe sings, "Look at me!"

We reach for tomatoes with quirky designs,
Each folly a treasure that brightly shines.
In this veggie patch, we celebrate,
A garden of giggles, a world first-rate.

So hoe and rake, let nonsense grow,
With every chuckle, let creativity flow.
Let's pluck those thoughts and toss them high,
In our field of laughs, give them wings to fly!

Nurturing the Untold

In a secret nook where whispers thrive,
Lies a world of stories eager to arrive.
Each untold tale dances in the night,
Seeking a friend, a curious light.

With a sprinkle of giggles and pots of cheer,
We nurture the laughter that draws them near.
"Tell me your secrets!" we coax with grins,
As characters tumble and laughter begins.

From the corners of joy, let's stock our shelves,
With tales of creatures who giggle themselves.
A cat in a hat, a fish on a bike,
Both spinning yarns that we all would like.

So gather round, let's make a feast,
Of tales that wiggle in every beast.
In the nurturing arms of whimsy and play,
We'll find treasures hidden, come join the fray!

The Spark Within

In the depths of my brain, a flicker ignites,
A dance of the neurons, like disco delights.
Ideas pop up, like corn in a pan,
All wiggly and giggly, here comes the plan!

I muse in the morning, with coffee in tow,
Contemplating pizza toppings, don't let me slow.
Each thought is a puppy, wagging its tail,
Chasing after nibbles, I can't seem to fail!

My mind's like a circus, a carnival spree,
Logic takes a nap, while the clowns sip on tea.
Muffins wear hats, and socks hold a chat,
In this funhouse of brains, where ideas go splat!

So here's to the madness, the silly, the bright,
Let creativity flourish, from day into night.
We'll gather our thoughts, like kids in a swing,
And laugh like hyenas, at the joy that we bring!

Petals of Insight

In the garden of ideas, bees buzz with glee,
Planting seeds of wisdom, as funny as can be.
Thistles wear tutus, while blooms join the play,
Whimsy runs rampant, all throughout the day!

A thought like a daisy pops up with a grin,
Whispering giggles, 'Oh, where do I begin?'
Tulips are chatting about clouds in the sky,
While laughing at daisies, 'Oh my, oh my!'

Rose bushes are rapping, each thorn knows its role,
Spinning wild tales, on a vegetable stroll.
Cabbages gossip in the shade, just for fun,
Debating if carrots can truly outrun!

The petals are twirling, a funny ballet,
Each vivid hue laughing, in jubilant display.
Let's pluck all our worries, create a bright rack,
In this festival of thoughts, we'll never look back!

In the Thicket of Thought

In a thicket of pondering, ideas take flight,
Squirrels barter wisdom, what a quirky sight!
Branches are trading, like stock on a spree,
While leaves toss around, 'What's the latest, you see?'

A wise old owl hoots, 'Be bold and be brash!'
'Make your own jelly, don't settle for trash!'
The bushes are chuckling, in silent delight,
As thoughts frolic freely, till they stagger from height!

We joke with the shadows, as they prance in the breeze,
Telling young ferns, 'Bring on the cheese!'
Ideas are wiggly, like worms in the dirt,
And views are so silly, they make my mind hurt!

So let's frolic together, and wiggle our minds,
In this thicket of giggles, some joy we will find.
We'll leap over logic, in bright colored boots,
And wade through the laughter, in tinfoil suits!

The Promise of Tomorrow

Tomorrow is waiting, in pajamas so bright,
Scribbling its dreams in the soft morning light.
Ideas tumble out, like socks in a load,
Each one has a story, each one hits the road!

With sunshine as our canvas, let's paint the day,
Pancakes are plotting a spectacular sway.
Butterflies chuckle, they know what we crave,
To dance in the airwaves, so silly and brave!

A toothbrush stands guard, with a toothy grin,
Encouraging smiles, 'Just let the fun in!'
The forecast says laughter, no clouds in the way,
While crayons discuss what they'll draw on this day!

So raise up your mugs, to tomorrows' delight,
Each giggle is precious, like stars in the night.
We'll twirl with our futures, with joy and a cheer,
In the promise of tomorrow, the laughter is clear!

www.ingramcontent.com/pod-product-compliance
Lightning Source LLC
Chambersburg PA
CBHW070312120526
44590CB00017B/2641